THIS NOTEBOOK
BELONGS TO

MONTHLY BUDGET

EXPENSES

MONTH

BUDGET

INCOME

TOTAL INCOME:

BILL TO BE PAID	DATE DUE	AMOUNT	PAID✓	NOTE
TOTAL				

MONTHLY BUDGET

OTHER EXPENSES	DATE	AMOUNT	NOTE
TOTAL			

TOTAL INCOME

TOTAL EXPENSES

DIFFERENCE

NOTES

WEEKLY EXPENSE TRACKER

MONTH ______

WEEK OF ______

BUDGET ______

MONDAY DATE ______

DESCRIPTION	AMOUNT
TOTAL	

TUESDAY DATE ______

DESCRIPTION	AMOUNT
TOTAL	

WEDNESDAY DATE ______

DESCRIPTION	AMOUNT
TOTAL	

THURSDAY DATE ______

DESCRIPTION	AMOUNT
TOTAL	

WEEKLY EXPENSE TRACKER

TOTAL EXPENSES

BALANCE

FRIDAY

DATE

DESCRIPTION	AMOUNT
TOTAL	

SATURDAY

DATE

DESCRIPTION	AMOUNT
TOTAL	

SUNDAY

DATE

DESCRIPTION	AMOUNT
TOTAL	

NOTES

WEEKLY EXPENSE TRACKER

MONTH ______________________

WEEK OF ______________________

BUDGET ______________________

MONDAY DATE ______________

DESCRIPTION	AMOUNT
TOTAL	

TUESDAY DATE ______________

DESCRIPTION	AMOUNT
TOTAL	

WEDNESDAY DATE ______________

DESCRIPTION	AMOUNT
TOTAL	

THURSDAY DATE ______________

DESCRIPTION	AMOUNT
TOTAL	

WEEKLY EXPENSE TRACKER

TOTAL EXPENSES

BALANCE

FRIDAY

DATE

DESCRIPTION	AMOUNT
TOTAL	

SATURDAY

DATE

DESCRIPTION	AMOUNT
TOTAL	

SUNDAY

DATE

DESCRIPTION	AMOUNT
TOTAL	

NOTES

WEEKLY EXPENSE TRACKER

MONTH

WEEK OF

BUDGET

MONDAY DATE

DESCRIPTION	AMOUNT
TOTAL	

TUESDAY DATE

DESCRIPTION	AMOUNT
TOTAL	

WEDNESDAY DATE

DESCRIPTION	AMOUNT
TOTAL	

THURSDAY DATE

DESCRIPTION	AMOUNT
TOTAL	

WEEKLY EXPENSE TRACKER

TOTAL EXPENSES

BALANCE

FRIDAY

DATE

DESCRIPTION	AMOUNT
TOTAL	

SATURDAY

DATE

DESCRIPTION	AMOUNT
TOTAL	

SUNDAY

DATE

DESCRIPTION	AMOUNT
TOTAL	

NOTES

WEEKLY EXPENSE TRACKER

MONTH

WEEK OF

BUDGET

MONDAY DATE

DESCRIPTION	AMOUNT
TOTAL	

TUESDAY DATE

DESCRIPTION	AMOUNT
TOTAL	

WEDNESDAY DATE

DESCRIPTION	AMOUNT
TOTAL	

THURSDAY DATE

DESCRIPTION	AMOUNT
TOTAL	

WEEKLY EXPENSE TRACKER

TOTAL EXPENSES ____________

BALANCE ____________

FRIDAY

DATE ____________

DESCRIPTION	AMOUNT
TOTAL	

SATURDAY

DATE ____________

DESCRIPTION	AMOUNT
TOTAL	

SUNDAY

DATE ____________

DESCRIPTION	AMOUNT
TOTAL	

NOTES

WEEKLY EXPENSE TRACKER

MONTH ______

WEEK OF ______

BUDGET ______

MONDAY DATE ______

DESCRIPTION	AMOUNT
TOTAL	

TUESDAY DATE ______

DESCRIPTION	AMOUNT
TOTAL	

WEDNESDAY DATE ______

DESCRIPTION	AMOUNT
TOTAL	

THURSDAY DATE ______

DESCRIPTION	AMOUNT
TOTAL	

WEEKLY EXPENSE TRACKER

TOTAL EXPENSES ____________________

BALANCE ____________________

FRIDAY

DATE ____________________

DESCRIPTION	AMOUNT
TOTAL	

SATURDAY

DATE ____________________

DESCRIPTION	AMOUNT
TOTAL	

SUNDAY

DATE ____________________

DESCRIPTION	AMOUNT
TOTAL	

NOTES

MONTHLY BUDGET

EXPENSES

MONTH

BUDGET

INCOME

TOTAL INCOME:

BILL TO BE PAID	DATE DUE	AMOUNT	PAID ✓	NOTE
TOTAL				

MONTHLY BUDGET

OTHER EXPENSES	DATE	AMOUNT	NOTE
TOTAL			

TOTAL INCOME

TOTAL EXPENSES

DIFFERENCE

NOTES

WEEKLY EXPENSE TRACKER

MONTH ______

WEEK OF ______

BUDGET ______

MONDAY DATE ______

DESCRIPTION	AMOUNT
TOTAL	

TUESDAY DATE ______

DESCRIPTION	AMOUNT
TOTAL	

WEDNESDAY DATE ______

DESCRIPTION	AMOUNT
TOTAL	

THURSDAY DATE ______

DESCRIPTION	AMOUNT
TOTAL	

WEEKLY EXPENSE TRACKER

TOTAL EXPENSES ____________________

BALANCE ____________________

FRIDAY

DATE ____________________

DESCRIPTION	AMOUNT
TOTAL	

SATURDAY

DATE ____________________

DESCRIPTION	AMOUNT
TOTAL	

SUNDAY

DATE ____________________

DESCRIPTION	AMOUNT
TOTAL	

NOTES

WEEKLY EXPENSE TRACKER

MONTH

WEEK OF

BUDGET

MONDAY DATE

DESCRIPTION	AMOUNT
TOTAL	

TUESDAY DATE

DESCRIPTION	AMOUNT
TOTAL	

WEDNESDAY DATE

DESCRIPTION	AMOUNT
TOTAL	

THURSDAY DATE

DESCRIPTION	AMOUNT
TOTAL	

WEEKLY EXPENSE TRACKER

TOTAL EXPENSES ______

BALANCE ______

FRIDAY DATE ______

DESCRIPTION	AMOUNT
TOTAL	

SATURDAY DATE ______

DESCRIPTION	AMOUNT
TOTAL	

SUNDAY DATE ______

DESCRIPTION	AMOUNT
TOTAL	

NOTES

WEEKLY EXPENSE TRACKER

MONTH

WEEK OF

BUDGET

MONDAY DATE

DESCRIPTION	AMOUNT
TOTAL	

TUESDAY DATE

DESCRIPTION	AMOUNT
TOTAL	

WEDNESDAY DATE

DESCRIPTION	AMOUNT
TOTAL	

THURSDAY DATE

DESCRIPTION	AMOUNT
TOTAL	

WEEKLY EXPENSE TRACKER

TOTAL EXPENSES

BALANCE

FRIDAY

DATE

DESCRIPTION	AMOUNT
TOTAL	

SATURDAY

DATE

DESCRIPTION	AMOUNT
TOTAL	

SUNDAY

DATE

DESCRIPTION	AMOUNT
TOTAL	

NOTES

WEEKLY EXPENSE TRACKER

MONTH ______________________

WEEK OF ______________________

BUDGET ______________________

MONDAY DATE ______________

DESCRIPTION	AMOUNT
TOTAL	

TUESDAY DATE ______________

DESCRIPTION	AMOUNT
TOTAL	

WEDNESDAY DATE ______________

DESCRIPTION	AMOUNT
TOTAL	

THURSDAY DATE ______________

DESCRIPTION	AMOUNT
TOTAL	

WEEKLY EXPENSE TRACKER

TOTAL EXPENSES

BALANCE

FRIDAY

DATE

DESCRIPTION	AMOUNT
TOTAL	

SATURDAY

DATE

DESCRIPTION	AMOUNT
TOTAL	

SUNDAY

DATE

DESCRIPTION	AMOUNT
TOTAL	

NOTES

WEEKLY EXPENSE TRACKER

MONTH

WEEK OF

BUDGET

MONDAY DATE

DESCRIPTION	AMOUNT
TOTAL	

TUESDAY DATE

DESCRIPTION	AMOUNT
TOTAL	

WEDNESDAY DATE

DESCRIPTION	AMOUNT
TOTAL	

THURSDAY DATE

DESCRIPTION	AMOUNT
TOTAL	

WEEKLY EXPENSE TRACKER

TOTAL EXPENSES ____________________

BALANCE ____________________

FRIDAY

DATE ____________________

DESCRIPTION	AMOUNT
TOTAL	

SATURDAY

DATE ____________________

DESCRIPTION	AMOUNT
TOTAL	

SUNDAY

DATE ____________________

DESCRIPTION	AMOUNT
TOTAL	

NOTES

MONTHLY BUDGET

EXPENSES

MONTH

BUDGET

INCOME

TOTAL INCOME:

BILL TO BE PAID	DATE DUE	AMOUNT	PAID✓	NOTE
TOTAL				

MONTHLY BUDGET

OTHER EXPENSES	DATE	AMOUNT	NOTE
TOTAL			

NOTES

TOTAL INCOME

TOTAL EXPENSES

DIFFERENCE

WEEKLY EXPENSE TRACKER

MONTH

WEEK OF

BUDGET

MONDAY DATE

DESCRIPTION	AMOUNT
TOTAL	

TUESDAY DATE

DESCRIPTION	AMOUNT
TOTAL	

WEDNESDAY DATE

DESCRIPTION	AMOUNT
TOTAL	

THURSDAY DATE

DESCRIPTION	AMOUNT
TOTAL	

WEEKLY EXPENSE TRACKER

TOTAL EXPENSES

BALANCE

FRIDAY

DATE

DESCRIPTION	AMOUNT
TOTAL	

SATURDAY

DATE

DESCRIPTION	AMOUNT
TOTAL	

SUNDAY

DATE

DESCRIPTION	AMOUNT
TOTAL	

NOTES

WEEKLY EXPENSE TRACKER

MONTH

WEEK OF

BUDGET

MONDAY DATE

DESCRIPTION	AMOUNT
TOTAL	

TUESDAY DATE

DESCRIPTION	AMOUNT
TOTAL	

WEDNESDAY DATE

DESCRIPTION	AMOUNT
TOTAL	

THURSDAY DATE

DESCRIPTION	AMOUNT
TOTAL	

WEEKLY EXPENSE TRACKER

TOTAL EXPENSES

BALANCE

FRIDAY

DATE

DESCRIPTION	AMOUNT
TOTAL	

SATURDAY

DATE

DESCRIPTION	AMOUNT
TOTAL	

SUNDAY

DATE

DESCRIPTION	AMOUNT
TOTAL	

NOTES

WEEKLY EXPENSE TRACKER

MONTH

WEEK OF

BUDGET

MONDAY DATE

DESCRIPTION	AMOUNT
TOTAL	

TUESDAY DATE

DESCRIPTION	AMOUNT
TOTAL	

WEDNESDAY DATE

DESCRIPTION	AMOUNT
TOTAL	

THURSDAY DATE

DESCRIPTION	AMOUNT
TOTAL	

WEEKLY EXPENSE TRACKER

TOTAL EXPENSES ______________

BALANCE ______________

FRIDAY

DATE ______________

DESCRIPTION	AMOUNT
TOTAL	

SATURDAY

DATE ______________

DESCRIPTION	AMOUNT
TOTAL	

SUNDAY

DATE ______________

DESCRIPTION	AMOUNT
TOTAL	

NOTES

WEEKLY EXPENSE TRACKER

MONTH ____

WEEK OF ____

BUDGET ____

MONDAY DATE ____

DESCRIPTION	AMOUNT
TOTAL	

TUESDAY DATE ____

DESCRIPTION	AMOUNT
TOTAL	

WEDNESDAY DATE ____

DESCRIPTION	AMOUNT
TOTAL	

THURSDAY DATE ____

DESCRIPTION	AMOUNT
TOTAL	

WEEKLY EXPENSE TRACKER

TOTAL EXPENSES

BALANCE

FRIDAY

DATE

DESCRIPTION	AMOUNT
TOTAL	

SATURDAY

DATE

DESCRIPTION	AMOUNT
TOTAL	

SUNDAY

DATE

DESCRIPTION	AMOUNT
TOTAL	

NOTES

WEEKLY EXPENSE TRACKER

MONTH

WEEK OF

BUDGET

MONDAY DATE

DESCRIPTION	AMOUNT
TOTAL	

TUESDAY DATE

DESCRIPTION	AMOUNT
TOTAL	

WEDNESDAY DATE

DESCRIPTION	AMOUNT
TOTAL	

THURSDAY DATE

DESCRIPTION	AMOUNT
TOTAL	

WEEKLY EXPENSE TRACKER

TOTAL EXPENSES ____________

BALANCE ____________

FRIDAY

DATE ____________

DESCRIPTION	AMOUNT
TOTAL	

SATURDAY

DATE ____________

DESCRIPTION	AMOUNT
TOTAL	

SUNDAY

DATE ____________

DESCRIPTION	AMOUNT
TOTAL	

NOTES

MONTHLY BUDGET

EXPENSES

MONTH

BUDGET

INCOME

TOTAL INCOME:

BILL TO BE PAID	DATE DUE	AMOUNT	PAID✓	NOTE
TOTAL				

MONTHLY BUDGET

OTHER EXPENSES	DATE	AMOUNT	NOTE
TOTAL			

TOTAL INCOME

TOTAL EXPENSES

DIFFERENCE

NOTES

WEEKLY EXPENSE TRACKER

MONTH ____________________

WEEK OF ____________________

BUDGET ____________________

MONDAY DATE ____________

DESCRIPTION	AMOUNT
TOTAL	

TUESDAY DATE ____________

DESCRIPTION	AMOUNT
TOTAL	

WEDNESDAY DATE ____________

DESCRIPTION	AMOUNT
TOTAL	

THURSDAY DATE ____________

DESCRIPTION	AMOUNT
TOTAL	

WEEKLY EXPENSE TRACKER

TOTAL EXPENSES

BALANCE

FRIDAY

DATE

DESCRIPTION	AMOUNT
TOTAL	

SATURDAY

DATE

DESCRIPTION	AMOUNT
TOTAL	

SUNDAY

DATE

DESCRIPTION	AMOUNT
TOTAL	

NOTES

WEEKLY EXPENSE TRACKER

MONTH

WEEK OF

BUDGET

MONDAY DATE

DESCRIPTION	AMOUNT
TOTAL	

TUESDAY DATE

DESCRIPTION	AMOUNT
TOTAL	

WEDNESDAY DATE

DESCRIPTION	AMOUNT
TOTAL	

THURSDAY DATE

DESCRIPTION	AMOUNT
TOTAL	

WEEKLY EXPENSE TRACKER

TOTAL EXPENSES

BALANCE

FRIDAY

DATE

DESCRIPTION	AMOUNT
TOTAL	

SATURDAY

DATE

DESCRIPTION	AMOUNT
TOTAL	

SUNDAY

DATE

DESCRIPTION	AMOUNT
TOTAL	

NOTES

WEEKLY EXPENSE TRACKER

MONTH

WEEK OF

BUDGET

MONDAY DATE

DESCRIPTION	AMOUNT
TOTAL	

TUESDAY DATE

DESCRIPTION	AMOUNT
TOTAL	

WEDNESDAY DATE

DESCRIPTION	AMOUNT
TOTAL	

THURSDAY DATE

DESCRIPTION	AMOUNT
TOTAL	

WEEKLY EXPENSE TRACKER

TOTAL EXPENSES

BALANCE

FRIDAY

DATE

DESCRIPTION	AMOUNT
TOTAL	

SATURDAY

DATE

DESCRIPTION	AMOUNT
TOTAL	

SUNDAY

DATE

DESCRIPTION	AMOUNT
TOTAL	

NOTES

WEEKLY EXPENSE TRACKER

MONTH

WEEK OF

BUDGET

MONDAY DATE

DESCRIPTION	AMOUNT
TOTAL	

TUESDAY DATE

DESCRIPTION	AMOUNT
TOTAL	

WEDNESDAY DATE

DESCRIPTION	AMOUNT
TOTAL	

THURSDAY DATE

DESCRIPTION	AMOUNT
TOTAL	

WEEKLY EXPENSE TRACKER

TOTAL EXPENSES

BALANCE

FRIDAY

DATE

DESCRIPTION	AMOUNT
TOTAL	

SATURDAY

DATE

DESCRIPTION	AMOUNT
TOTAL	

SUNDAY

DATE

DESCRIPTION	AMOUNT
TOTAL	

NOTES

WEEKLY EXPENSE TRACKER

MONTH

WEEK OF

BUDGET

MONDAY DATE

DESCRIPTION	AMOUNT
TOTAL	

TUESDAY DATE

DESCRIPTION	AMOUNT
TOTAL	

WEDNESDAY DATE

DESCRIPTION	AMOUNT
TOTAL	

THURSDAY DATE

DESCRIPTION	AMOUNT
TOTAL	

WEEKLY EXPENSE TRACKER

TOTAL EXPENSES ____________

BALANCE ____________

FRIDAY DATE ____________

DESCRIPTION	AMOUNT
TOTAL	

SATURDAY DATE ____________

DESCRIPTION	AMOUNT
TOTAL	

SUNDAY DATE ____________

DESCRIPTION	AMOUNT
TOTAL	

NOTES

MONTHLY BUDGET

EXPENSES

MONTH

BUDGET

INCOME

TOTAL INCOME:

BILL TO BE PAID	DATE DUE	AMOUNT	PAID✓	NOTE
TOTAL				

MONTHLY BUDGET

OTHER EXPENSES	DATE	AMOUNT	NOTE
TOTAL			

TOTAL INCOME

TOTAL EXPENSES

DIFFERENCE

NOTES

WEEKLY EXPENSE TRACKER

MONTH
WEEK OF
BUDGET

MONDAY DATE

DESCRIPTION	AMOUNT
TOTAL	

TUESDAY DATE

DESCRIPTION	AMOUNT
TOTAL	

WEDNESDAY DATE

DESCRIPTION	AMOUNT
TOTAL	

THURSDAY DATE

DESCRIPTION	AMOUNT
TOTAL	

WEEKLY EXPENSE TRACKER

TOTAL EXPENSES

BALANCE

FRIDAY

DATE

DESCRIPTION	AMOUNT
TOTAL	

SATURDAY

DATE

DESCRIPTION	AMOUNT
TOTAL	

SUNDAY

DATE

DESCRIPTION	AMOUNT
TOTAL	

NOTES

WEEKLY EXPENSE TRACKER

MONTH

WEEK OF

BUDGET

MONDAY DATE

DESCRIPTION	AMOUNT
TOTAL	

TUESDAY DATE

DESCRIPTION	AMOUNT
TOTAL	

WEDNESDAY DATE

DESCRIPTION	AMOUNT
TOTAL	

THURSDAY DATE

DESCRIPTION	AMOUNT
TOTAL	

WEEKLY EXPENSE TRACKER

TOTAL EXPENSES

BALANCE

FRIDAY

DATE

DESCRIPTION	AMOUNT
TOTAL	

SATURDAY

DATE

DESCRIPTION	AMOUNT
TOTAL	

SUNDAY

DATE

DESCRIPTION	AMOUNT
TOTAL	

NOTES

WEEKLY EXPENSE TRACKER

MONTH

WEEK OF

BUDGET

MONDAY DATE

DESCRIPTION	AMOUNT
TOTAL	

TUESDAY DATE

DESCRIPTION	AMOUNT
TOTAL	

WEDNESDAY DATE

DESCRIPTION	AMOUNT
TOTAL	

THURSDAY DATE

DESCRIPTION	AMOUNT
TOTAL	

WEEKLY EXPENSE TRACKER

TOTAL EXPENSES

BALANCE

FRIDAY

DATE

DESCRIPTION	AMOUNT
TOTAL	

SATURDAY

DATE

DESCRIPTION	AMOUNT
TOTAL	

SUNDAY

DATE

DESCRIPTION	AMOUNT
TOTAL	

NOTES

WEEKLY EXPENSE TRACKER

MONTH

WEEK OF

BUDGET

MONDAY DATE

DESCRIPTION	AMOUNT
TOTAL	

TUESDAY DATE

DESCRIPTION	AMOUNT
TOTAL	

WEDNESDAY DATE

DESCRIPTION	AMOUNT
TOTAL	

THURSDAY DATE

DESCRIPTION	AMOUNT
TOTAL	

WEEKLY EXPENSE TRACKER

TOTAL EXPENSES

BALANCE

FRIDAY DATE

DESCRIPTION	AMOUNT
TOTAL	

SATURDAY DATE

DESCRIPTION	AMOUNT
TOTAL	

SUNDAY DATE

DESCRIPTION	AMOUNT
TOTAL	

NOTES

WEEKLY EXPENSE TRACKER

MONTH

WEEK OF

BUDGET

MONDAY DATE

DESCRIPTION	AMOUNT
TOTAL	

TUESDAY DATE

DESCRIPTION	AMOUNT
TOTAL	

WEDNESDAY DATE

DESCRIPTION	AMOUNT
TOTAL	

THURSDAY DATE

DESCRIPTION	AMOUNT
TOTAL	

WEEKLY EXPENSE TRACKER

TOTAL EXPENSES

BALANCE

FRIDAY

DATE

DESCRIPTION	AMOUNT
TOTAL	

SATURDAY

DATE

DESCRIPTION	AMOUNT
TOTAL	

SUNDAY

DATE

DESCRIPTION	AMOUNT
TOTAL	

NOTES

MONTHLY BUDGET

EXPENSES

MONTH

BUDGET

INCOME

TOTAL INCOME:

BILL TO BE PAID	DATE DUE	AMOUNT	PAID✓	NOTE
TOTAL				

MONTHLY BUDGET

OTHER EXPENSES	DATE	AMOUNT	NOTE
TOTAL			

TOTAL INCOME

TOTAL EXPENSES

DIFFERENCE

NOTES

WEEKLY EXPENSE TRACKER

MONTH

WEEK OF

BUDGET

MONDAY DATE

DESCRIPTION	AMOUNT
TOTAL	

TUESDAY DATE

DESCRIPTION	AMOUNT
TOTAL	

WEDNESDAY DATE

DESCRIPTION	AMOUNT
TOTAL	

THURSDAY DATE

DESCRIPTION	AMOUNT
TOTAL	

WEEKLY EXPENSE TRACKER

TOTAL EXPENSES

BALANCE

FRIDAY

DATE

DESCRIPTION	AMOUNT
TOTAL	

SATURDAY

DATE

DESCRIPTION	AMOUNT
TOTAL	

SUNDAY

DATE

DESCRIPTION	AMOUNT
TOTAL	

NOTES

WEEKLY EXPENSE TRACKER

MONTH

WEEK OF

BUDGET

MONDAY DATE

DESCRIPTION	AMOUNT
TOTAL	

TUESDAY DATE

DESCRIPTION	AMOUNT
TOTAL	

WEDNESDAY DATE

DESCRIPTION	AMOUNT
TOTAL	

THURSDAY DATE

DESCRIPTION	AMOUNT
TOTAL	

WEEKLY EXPENSE TRACKER

TOTAL EXPENSES

BALANCE

FRIDAY

DATE

DESCRIPTION	AMOUNT
TOTAL	

SATURDAY

DATE

DESCRIPTION	AMOUNT
TOTAL	

SUNDAY

DATE

DESCRIPTION	AMOUNT
TOTAL	

NOTES

WEEKLY EXPENSE TRACKER

MONTH

WEEK OF

BUDGET

MONDAY

DATE

DESCRIPTION	AMOUNT
TOTAL	

TUESDAY

DATE

DESCRIPTION	AMOUNT
TOTAL	

WEDNESDAY

DATE

DESCRIPTION	AMOUNT
TOTAL	

THURSDAY

DATE

DESCRIPTION	AMOUNT
TOTAL	

WEEKLY EXPENSE TRACKER

TOTAL EXPENSES ____________

BALANCE ____________

FRIDAY DATE ____________

DESCRIPTION	AMOUNT
TOTAL	

SATURDAY DATE ____________

DESCRIPTION	AMOUNT
TOTAL	

SUNDAY DATE ____________

DESCRIPTION	AMOUNT
TOTAL	

NOTES

WEEKLY EXPENSE TRACKER

MONTH

WEEK OF

BUDGET

MONDAY DATE

DESCRIPTION	AMOUNT
TOTAL	

TUESDAY DATE

DESCRIPTION	AMOUNT
TOTAL	

WEDNESDAY DATE

DESCRIPTION	AMOUNT
TOTAL	

THURSDAY DATE

DESCRIPTION	AMOUNT
TOTAL	

WEEKLY EXPENSE TRACKER

TOTAL EXPENSES

BALANCE

FRIDAY

DATE

DESCRIPTION	AMOUNT
TOTAL	

SATURDAY

DATE

DESCRIPTION	AMOUNT
TOTAL	

SUNDAY

DATE

DESCRIPTION	AMOUNT
TOTAL	

NOTES

WEEKLY EXPENSE TRACKER

MONTH ____________________

WEEK OF ____________________

BUDGET ____________________

MONDAY DATE ____________

DESCRIPTION	AMOUNT
TOTAL	

TUESDAY DATE ____________

DESCRIPTION	AMOUNT
TOTAL	

WEDNESDAY DATE ____________

DESCRIPTION	AMOUNT
TOTAL	

THURSDAY DATE ____________

DESCRIPTION	AMOUNT
TOTAL	

WEEKLY EXPENSE TRACKER

TOTAL EXPENSES

BALANCE

FRIDAY
DATE

DESCRIPTION	AMOUNT
TOTAL	

SATURDAY
DATE

DESCRIPTION	AMOUNT
TOTAL	

SUNDAY
DATE

DESCRIPTION	AMOUNT
TOTAL	

NOTES

MONTHLY BUDGET

EXPENSES

MONTH

BUDGET

INCOME

TOTAL INCOME:

BILL TO BE PAID	DATE DUE	AMOUNT	PAID✓	NOTE
TOTAL				

MONTHLY BUDGET

OTHER EXPENSES	DATE	AMOUNT	NOTE
TOTAL			

NOTES

TOTAL INCOME

TOTAL EXPENSES

DIFFERENCE

WEEKLY EXPENSE TRACKER

MONTH

WEEK OF

BUDGET

MONDAY DATE

DESCRIPTION	AMOUNT
TOTAL	

TUESDAY DATE

DESCRIPTION	AMOUNT
TOTAL	

WEDNESDAY DATE

DESCRIPTION	AMOUNT
TOTAL	

THURSDAY DATE

DESCRIPTION	AMOUNT
TOTAL	

WEEKLY EXPENSE TRACKER

TOTAL EXPENSES

BALANCE

FRIDAY

DATE

DESCRIPTION	AMOUNT
TOTAL	

SATURDAY

DATE

DESCRIPTION	AMOUNT
TOTAL	

SUNDAY

DATE

DESCRIPTION	AMOUNT
TOTAL	

NOTES

WEEKLY EXPENSE TRACKER

MONTH ____

WEEK OF ____

BUDGET ____

MONDAY DATE ____

DESCRIPTION	AMOUNT
TOTAL	

TUESDAY DATE ____

DESCRIPTION	AMOUNT
TOTAL	

WEDNESDAY DATE ____

DESCRIPTION	AMOUNT
TOTAL	

THURSDAY DATE ____

DESCRIPTION	AMOUNT
TOTAL	

WEEKLY EXPENSE TRACKER

TOTAL EXPENSES

BALANCE

FRIDAY

DATE

DESCRIPTION	AMOUNT
TOTAL	

SATURDAY

DATE

DESCRIPTION	AMOUNT
TOTAL	

SUNDAY

DATE

DESCRIPTION	AMOUNT
TOTAL	

NOTES

WEEKLY EXPENSE TRACKER

MONTH ______

WEEK OF ______

BUDGET ______

MONDAY DATE ______

DESCRIPTION	AMOUNT
TOTAL	

TUESDAY DATE ______

DESCRIPTION	AMOUNT
TOTAL	

WEDNESDAY DATE ______

DESCRIPTION	AMOUNT
TOTAL	

THURSDAY DATE ______

DESCRIPTION	AMOUNT
TOTAL	

WEEKLY EXPENSE TRACKER

TOTAL EXPENSES ____________________

BALANCE ____________________

FRIDAY DATE ____________________

DESCRIPTION	AMOUNT
TOTAL	

SATURDAY DATE ____________________

DESCRIPTION	AMOUNT
TOTAL	

SUNDAY DATE ____________________

DESCRIPTION	AMOUNT
TOTAL	

NOTES

WEEKLY EXPENSE TRACKER

MONTH ______

WEEK OF ______

BUDGET ______

MONDAY DATE ______

DESCRIPTION	AMOUNT
TOTAL	

TUESDAY DATE ______

DESCRIPTION	AMOUNT
TOTAL	

WEDNESDAY DATE ______

DESCRIPTION	AMOUNT
TOTAL	

THURSDAY DATE ______

DESCRIPTION	AMOUNT
TOTAL	

WEEKLY EXPENSE TRACKER

TOTAL EXPENSES

BALANCE

FRIDAY

DATE

DESCRIPTION	AMOUNT
TOTAL	

SATURDAY

DATE

DESCRIPTION	AMOUNT
TOTAL	

SUNDAY

DATE

DESCRIPTION	AMOUNT
TOTAL	

NOTES

WEEKLY EXPENSE TRACKER

MONTH

WEEK OF

BUDGET

MONDAY DATE

DESCRIPTION	AMOUNT
TOTAL	

TUESDAY DATE

DESCRIPTION	AMOUNT
TOTAL	

WEDNESDAY DATE

DESCRIPTION	AMOUNT
TOTAL	

THURSDAY DATE

DESCRIPTION	AMOUNT
TOTAL	

WEEKLY EXPENSE TRACKER

TOTAL EXPENSES

BALANCE

FRIDAY

DATE

DESCRIPTION	AMOUNT
TOTAL	

SATURDAY

DATE

DESCRIPTION	AMOUNT
TOTAL	

SUNDAY

DATE

DESCRIPTION	AMOUNT
TOTAL	

NOTES

MONTHLY BUDGET

EXPENSES

MONTH

BUDGET

INCOME

TOTAL INCOME:

BILL TO BE PAID	DATE DUE	AMOUNT	PAID✓	NOTE
TOTAL				

MONTHLY BUDGET

OTHER EXPENSES	DATE	AMOUNT	NOTE
TOTAL			

NOTES

TOTAL INCOME

TOTAL EXPENSES

DIFFERENCE

WEEKLY EXPENSE TRACKER

MONTH

WEEK OF

BUDGET

MONDAY DATE

DESCRIPTION	AMOUNT
TOTAL	

TUESDAY DATE

DESCRIPTION	AMOUNT
TOTAL	

WEDNESDAY DATE

DESCRIPTION	AMOUNT
TOTAL	

THURSDAY DATE

DESCRIPTION	AMOUNT
TOTAL	

WEEKLY EXPENSE TRACKER

TOTAL EXPENSES ____________________

BALANCE ____________________

FRIDAY

DATE ____________________

DESCRIPTION	AMOUNT
TOTAL	

SATURDAY

DATE ____________________

DESCRIPTION	AMOUNT
TOTAL	

SUNDAY

DATE ____________________

DESCRIPTION	AMOUNT
TOTAL	

NOTES

WEEKLY EXPENSE TRACKER

MONTH

WEEK OF

BUDGET

MONDAY DATE

DESCRIPTION	AMOUNT
TOTAL	

TUESDAY DATE

DESCRIPTION	AMOUNT
TOTAL	

WEDNESDAY DATE

DESCRIPTION	AMOUNT
TOTAL	

THURSDAY DATE

DESCRIPTION	AMOUNT
TOTAL	

WEEKLY EXPENSE TRACKER

TOTAL EXPENSES

BALANCE

FRIDAY

DATE

DESCRIPTION	AMOUNT
TOTAL	

SATURDAY

DATE

DESCRIPTION	AMOUNT
TOTAL	

SUNDAY

DATE

DESCRIPTION	AMOUNT
TOTAL	

NOTES

WEEKLY EXPENSE TRACKER

MONTH

WEEK OF

BUDGET

MONDAY DATE

DESCRIPTION	AMOUNT
TOTAL	

TUESDAY DATE

DESCRIPTION	AMOUNT
TOTAL	

WEDNESDAY DATE

DESCRIPTION	AMOUNT
TOTAL	

THURSDAY DATE

DESCRIPTION	AMOUNT
TOTAL	

WEEKLY EXPENSE TRACKER

TOTAL EXPENSES

BALANCE

FRIDAY DATE

DESCRIPTION	AMOUNT
TOTAL	

SATURDAY DATE

DESCRIPTION	AMOUNT
TOTAL	

SUNDAY DATE

DESCRIPTION	AMOUNT
TOTAL	

NOTES

WEEKLY EXPENSE TRACKER

MONTH

WEEK OF

BUDGET

MONDAY DATE

DESCRIPTION	AMOUNT
TOTAL	

TUESDAY DATE

DESCRIPTION	AMOUNT
TOTAL	

WEDNESDAY DATE

DESCRIPTION	AMOUNT
TOTAL	

THURSDAY DATE

DESCRIPTION	AMOUNT
TOTAL	

WEEKLY EXPENSE TRACKER

TOTAL EXPENSES ____________________

BALANCE ____________________

FRIDAY

DATE ____________________

DESCRIPTION	AMOUNT
TOTAL	

SATURDAY

DATE ____________________

DESCRIPTION	AMOUNT
TOTAL	

SUNDAY

DATE ____________________

DESCRIPTION	AMOUNT
TOTAL	

NOTES

WEEKLY EXPENSE TRACKER

MONTH ______
WEEK OF ______
BUDGET ______

MONDAY DATE ______

DESCRIPTION	AMOUNT
TOTAL	

TUESDAY DATE ______

DESCRIPTION	AMOUNT
TOTAL	

WEDNESDAY DATE ______

DESCRIPTION	AMOUNT
TOTAL	

THURSDAY DATE ______

DESCRIPTION	AMOUNT
TOTAL	

WEEKLY EXPENSE TRACKER

TOTAL EXPENSES

BALANCE

FRIDAY

DATE

DESCRIPTION	AMOUNT
TOTAL	

SATURDAY

DATE

DESCRIPTION	AMOUNT
TOTAL	

SUNDAY

DATE

DESCRIPTION	AMOUNT
TOTAL	

NOTES

MONTHLY BUDGET

EXPENSES

MONTH

BUDGET

INCOME

TOTAL INCOME:

BILL TO BE PAID	DATE DUE	AMOUNT	PAID✓	NOTE
TOTAL				

MONTHLY BUDGET

OTHER EXPENSES	DATE	AMOUNT	NOTE
TOTAL			

NOTES

TOTAL INCOME

TOTAL EXPENSES

DIFFERENCE

WEEKLY EXPENSE TRACKER

MONTH ______

WEEK OF ______

BUDGET ______

MONDAY DATE ______

DESCRIPTION	AMOUNT
TOTAL	

TUESDAY DATE ______

DESCRIPTION	AMOUNT
TOTAL	

WEDNESDAY DATE ______

DESCRIPTION	AMOUNT
TOTAL	

THURSDAY DATE ______

DESCRIPTION	AMOUNT
TOTAL	

WEEKLY EXPENSE TRACKER

TOTAL EXPENSES

BALANCE

FRIDAY

DATE

DESCRIPTION	AMOUNT
TOTAL	

SATURDAY

DATE

DESCRIPTION	AMOUNT
TOTAL	

SUNDAY

DATE

DESCRIPTION	AMOUNT
TOTAL	

NOTES

WEEKLY EXPENSE TRACKER

MONTH ______________________

WEEK OF ______________________

BUDGET ______________________

MONDAY DATE ______________

DESCRIPTION	AMOUNT
TOTAL	

TUESDAY DATE ______________

DESCRIPTION	AMOUNT
TOTAL	

WEDNESDAY DATE ______________

DESCRIPTION	AMOUNT
TOTAL	

THURSDAY DATE ______________

DESCRIPTION	AMOUNT
TOTAL	

WEEKLY EXPENSE TRACKER

TOTAL EXPENSES

BALANCE

FRIDAY

DATE

DESCRIPTION	AMOUNT
TOTAL	

SATURDAY

DATE

DESCRIPTION	AMOUNT
TOTAL	

SUNDAY

DATE

DESCRIPTION	AMOUNT
TOTAL	

NOTES

WEEKLY EXPENSE TRACKER

MONTH

WEEK OF

BUDGET

MONDAY DATE

DESCRIPTION	AMOUNT
TOTAL	

TUESDAY DATE

DESCRIPTION	AMOUNT
TOTAL	

WEDNESDAY DATE

DESCRIPTION	AMOUNT
TOTAL	

THURSDAY DATE

DESCRIPTION	AMOUNT
TOTAL	

WEEKLY EXPENSE TRACKER

TOTAL EXPENSES

BALANCE

FRIDAY

DATE

DESCRIPTION	AMOUNT
TOTAL	

SATURDAY

DATE

DESCRIPTION	AMOUNT
TOTAL	

SUNDAY

DATE

DESCRIPTION	AMOUNT
TOTAL	

NOTES

WEEKLY EXPENSE TRACKER

MONTH

WEEK OF

BUDGET

MONDAY DATE

DESCRIPTION	AMOUNT
TOTAL	

TUESDAY DATE

DESCRIPTION	AMOUNT
TOTAL	

WEDNESDAY DATE

DESCRIPTION	AMOUNT
TOTAL	

THURSDAY DATE

DESCRIPTION	AMOUNT
TOTAL	

WEEKLY EXPENSE TRACKER

TOTAL EXPENSES ______

BALANCE ______

FRIDAY
DATE ______

DESCRIPTION	AMOUNT
TOTAL	

SATURDAY
DATE ______

DESCRIPTION	AMOUNT
TOTAL	

SUNDAY
DATE ______

DESCRIPTION	AMOUNT
TOTAL	

NOTES

WEEKLY EXPENSE TRACKER

MONTH

WEEK OF

BUDGET

MONDAY DATE

DESCRIPTION	AMOUNT
TOTAL	

TUESDAY DATE

DESCRIPTION	AMOUNT
TOTAL	

WEDNESDAY DATE

DESCRIPTION	AMOUNT
TOTAL	

THURSDAY DATE

DESCRIPTION	AMOUNT
TOTAL	

WEEKLY EXPENSE TRACKER

TOTAL EXPENSES

BALANCE

FRIDAY

DATE

DESCRIPTION	AMOUNT
TOTAL	

SATURDAY

DATE

DESCRIPTION	AMOUNT
TOTAL	

SUNDAY

DATE

DESCRIPTION	AMOUNT
TOTAL	

NOTES

MONTHLY BUDGET

EXPENSES

MONTH ______________

BUDGET ______________

INCOME
____
____
____
____
____
____

TOTAL INCOME: ______________

BILL TO BE PAID	DATE DUE	AMOUNT	PAID✓	NOTE
TOTAL				

MONTHLY BUDGET

OTHER EXPENSES	DATE	AMOUNT	NOTE
TOTAL			

TOTAL INCOME

TOTAL EXPENSES

DIFFERENCE

NOTES

WEEKLY EXPENSE TRACKER

MONTH ____________

WEEK OF ____________

BUDGET ____________

MONDAY DATE ____________

DESCRIPTION	AMOUNT
TOTAL	

TUESDAY DATE ____________

DESCRIPTION	AMOUNT
TOTAL	

WEDNESDAY DATE ____________

DESCRIPTION	AMOUNT
TOTAL	

THURSDAY DATE ____________

DESCRIPTION	AMOUNT
TOTAL	

WEEKLY EXPENSE TRACKER

TOTAL EXPENSES

BALANCE

FRIDAY

DATE

DESCRIPTION	AMOUNT
TOTAL	

SATURDAY

DATE

DESCRIPTION	AMOUNT
TOTAL	

SUNDAY

DATE

DESCRIPTION	AMOUNT
TOTAL	

NOTES

WEEKLY EXPENSE TRACKER

MONTH

WEEK OF

BUDGET

MONDAY DATE

DESCRIPTION	AMOUNT
TOTAL	

TUESDAY DATE

DESCRIPTION	AMOUNT
TOTAL	

WEDNESDAY DATE

DESCRIPTION	AMOUNT
TOTAL	

THURSDAY DATE

DESCRIPTION	AMOUNT
TOTAL	

WEEKLY EXPENSE TRACKER

TOTAL EXPENSES

BALANCE

FRIDAY

DATE

DESCRIPTION	AMOUNT
TOTAL	

SATURDAY

DATE

DESCRIPTION	AMOUNT
TOTAL	

SUNDAY

DATE

DESCRIPTION	AMOUNT
TOTAL	

NOTES

WEEKLY EXPENSE TRACKER

MONTH ____________________

WEEK OF ____________________

BUDGET ____________________

MONDAY DATE ____________

DESCRIPTION	AMOUNT
TOTAL	

TUESDAY DATE ____________

DESCRIPTION	AMOUNT
TOTAL	

WEDNESDAY DATE ____________

DESCRIPTION	AMOUNT
TOTAL	

THURSDAY DATE ____________

DESCRIPTION	AMOUNT
TOTAL	

WEEKLY EXPENSE TRACKER

TOTAL EXPENSES

BALANCE

FRIDAY

DATE

DESCRIPTION	AMOUNT
TOTAL	

SATURDAY

DATE

DESCRIPTION	AMOUNT
TOTAL	

SUNDAY

DATE

DESCRIPTION	AMOUNT
TOTAL	

NOTES

WEEKLY EXPENSE TRACKER

MONTH

WEEK OF

BUDGET

MONDAY DATE

DESCRIPTION	AMOUNT
TOTAL	

TUESDAY DATE

DESCRIPTION	AMOUNT
TOTAL	

WEDNESDAY DATE

DESCRIPTION	AMOUNT
TOTAL	

THURSDAY DATE

DESCRIPTION	AMOUNT
TOTAL	

WEEKLY EXPENSE TRACKER

TOTAL EXPENSES ______

BALANCE ______

FRIDAY DATE ______

DESCRIPTION	AMOUNT
TOTAL	

SATURDAY DATE ______

DESCRIPTION	AMOUNT
TOTAL	

SUNDAY DATE ______

DESCRIPTION	AMOUNT
TOTAL	

NOTES

WEEKLY EXPENSE TRACKER

MONTH ____________

WEEK OF ____________

BUDGET ____________

MONDAY DATE ____________

DESCRIPTION	AMOUNT
TOTAL	

TUESDAY DATE ____________

DESCRIPTION	AMOUNT
TOTAL	

WEDNESDAY DATE ____________

DESCRIPTION	AMOUNT
TOTAL	

THURSDAY DATE ____________

DESCRIPTION	AMOUNT
TOTAL	

WEEKLY EXPENSE TRACKER

TOTAL EXPENSES

BALANCE

FRIDAY

DATE

DESCRIPTION	AMOUNT
TOTAL	

SATURDAY

DATE

DESCRIPTION	AMOUNT
TOTAL	

SUNDAY

DATE

DESCRIPTION	AMOUNT
TOTAL	

NOTES

MONTHLY BUDGET

EXPENSES

MONTH

BUDGET

INCOME

TOTAL INCOME:

BILL TO BE PAID	DATE DUE	AMOUNT	PAID✓	NOTE
TOTAL				

MONTHLY BUDGET

OTHER EXPENSES	DATE	AMOUNT	NOTE
TOTAL			

TOTAL INCOME

TOTAL EXPENSES

DIFFERENCE

NOTES

WEEKLY EXPENSE TRACKER

MONTH

WEEK OF

BUDGET

MONDAY DATE

DESCRIPTION	AMOUNT
TOTAL	

TUESDAY DATE

DESCRIPTION	AMOUNT
TOTAL	

WEDNESDAY DATE

DESCRIPTION	AMOUNT
TOTAL	

THURSDAY DATE

DESCRIPTION	AMOUNT
TOTAL	

WEEKLY EXPENSE TRACKER

TOTAL EXPENSES

BALANCE

FRIDAY

DATE

DESCRIPTION	AMOUNT
TOTAL	

SATURDAY

DATE

DESCRIPTION	AMOUNT
TOTAL	

SUNDAY

DATE

DESCRIPTION	AMOUNT
TOTAL	

NOTES

WEEKLY EXPENSE TRACKER

MONTH

WEEK OF

BUDGET

MONDAY DATE

DESCRIPTION	AMOUNT
TOTAL	

TUESDAY DATE

DESCRIPTION	AMOUNT
TOTAL	

WEDNESDAY DATE

DESCRIPTION	AMOUNT
TOTAL	

THURSDAY DATE

DESCRIPTION	AMOUNT
TOTAL	

WEEKLY EXPENSE TRACKER

TOTAL EXPENSES

BALANCE

FRIDAY DATE

DESCRIPTION	AMOUNT
TOTAL	

SATURDAY DATE

DESCRIPTION	AMOUNT
TOTAL	

SUNDAY DATE

DESCRIPTION	AMOUNT
TOTAL	

NOTES

WEEKLY EXPENSE TRACKER

MONTH

WEEK OF

BUDGET

MONDAY DATE

DESCRIPTION	AMOUNT
TOTAL	

TUESDAY DATE

DESCRIPTION	AMOUNT
TOTAL	

WEDNESDAY DATE

DESCRIPTION	AMOUNT
TOTAL	

THURSDAY DATE

DESCRIPTION	AMOUNT
TOTAL	

WEEKLY EXPENSE TRACKER

TOTAL EXPENSES

BALANCE

FRIDAY DATE

DESCRIPTION	AMOUNT
TOTAL	

SATURDAY DATE

DESCRIPTION	AMOUNT
TOTAL	

SUNDAY DATE

DESCRIPTION	AMOUNT
TOTAL	

NOTES

WEEKLY EXPENSE TRACKER

MONTH

WEEK OF

BUDGET

MONDAY DATE

DESCRIPTION	AMOUNT
TOTAL	

TUESDAY DATE

DESCRIPTION	AMOUNT
TOTAL	

WEDNESDAY DATE

DESCRIPTION	AMOUNT
TOTAL	

THURSDAY DATE

DESCRIPTION	AMOUNT
TOTAL	

WEEKLY EXPENSE TRACKER

TOTAL EXPENSES ____________

BALANCE ____________

FRIDAY

DATE ____________

DESCRIPTION	AMOUNT
TOTAL	

SATURDAY

DATE ____________

DESCRIPTION	AMOUNT
TOTAL	

SUNDAY

DATE ____________

DESCRIPTION	AMOUNT
TOTAL	

NOTES

WEEKLY EXPENSE TRACKER

MONTH ____________

WEEK OF ____________

BUDGET ____________

MONDAY DATE ____________

DESCRIPTION	AMOUNT
TOTAL	

TUESDAY DATE ____________

DESCRIPTION	AMOUNT
TOTAL	

WEDNESDAY DATE ____________

DESCRIPTION	AMOUNT
TOTAL	

THURSDAY DATE ____________

DESCRIPTION	AMOUNT
TOTAL	

WEEKLY EXPENSE TRACKER

TOTAL EXPENSES

BALANCE

FRIDAY

DATE

DESCRIPTION	AMOUNT
TOTAL	

SATURDAY

DATE

DESCRIPTION	AMOUNT
TOTAL	

SUNDAY

DATE

DESCRIPTION	AMOUNT
TOTAL	

NOTES

MONTHLY BUDGET

EXPENSES

MONTH

BUDGET

INCOME

TOTAL INCOME:

BILL TO BE PAID	DATE DUE	AMOUNT	PAID✓	NOTE
TOTAL				

MONTHLY BUDGET

OTHER EXPENSES	DATE	AMOUNT	NOTE
TOTAL			

TOTAL INCOME

TOTAL EXPENSES

DIFFERENCE

NOTES

WEEKLY EXPENSE TRACKER

MONTH

WEEK OF

BUDGET

MONDAY

DATE

DESCRIPTION	AMOUNT
TOTAL	

TUESDAY

DATE

DESCRIPTION	AMOUNT
TOTAL	

WEDNESDAY

DATE

DESCRIPTION	AMOUNT
TOTAL	

THURSDAY

DATE

DESCRIPTION	AMOUNT
TOTAL	

WEEKLY EXPENSE TRACKER

TOTAL EXPENSES

BALANCE

FRIDAY

DATE

DESCRIPTION	AMOUNT
TOTAL	

SATURDAY

DATE

DESCRIPTION	AMOUNT
TOTAL	

SUNDAY

DATE

DESCRIPTION	AMOUNT
TOTAL	

NOTES

WEEKLY EXPENSE TRACKER

MONTH

WEEK OF

BUDGET

MONDAY DATE

DESCRIPTION	AMOUNT
TOTAL	

TUESDAY DATE

DESCRIPTION	AMOUNT
TOTAL	

WEDNESDAY DATE

DESCRIPTION	AMOUNT
TOTAL	

THURSDAY DATE

DESCRIPTION	AMOUNT
TOTAL	

WEEKLY EXPENSE TRACKER

TOTAL EXPENSES

BALANCE

FRIDAY

DATE

DESCRIPTION	AMOUNT
TOTAL	

SATURDAY

DATE

DESCRIPTION	AMOUNT
TOTAL	

SUNDAY

DATE

DESCRIPTION	AMOUNT
TOTAL	

NOTES

WEEKLY EXPENSE TRACKER

MONTH

WEEK OF

BUDGET

MONDAY DATE

DESCRIPTION	AMOUNT
TOTAL	

TUESDAY DATE

DESCRIPTION	AMOUNT
TOTAL	

WEDNESDAY DATE

DESCRIPTION	AMOUNT
TOTAL	

THURSDAY DATE

DESCRIPTION	AMOUNT
TOTAL	

WEEKLY EXPENSE TRACKER

TOTAL EXPENSES ____________

BALANCE ____________

FRIDAY DATE ____________

DESCRIPTION	AMOUNT
TOTAL	

SATURDAY DATE ____________

DESCRIPTION	AMOUNT
TOTAL	

SUNDAY DATE ____________

DESCRIPTION	AMOUNT
TOTAL	

NOTES

WEEKLY EXPENSE TRACKER

MONTH

WEEK OF

BUDGET

MONDAY DATE

DESCRIPTION	AMOUNT
TOTAL	

TUESDAY DATE

DESCRIPTION	AMOUNT
TOTAL	

WEDNESDAY DATE

DESCRIPTION	AMOUNT
TOTAL	

THURSDAY DATE

DESCRIPTION	AMOUNT
TOTAL	

WEEKLY EXPENSE TRACKER

TOTAL EXPENSES ____________

BALANCE ____________

FRIDAY DATE ____________

DESCRIPTION	AMOUNT
TOTAL	

SATURDAY DATE ____________

DESCRIPTION	AMOUNT
TOTAL	

SUNDAY DATE ____________

DESCRIPTION	AMOUNT
TOTAL	

NOTES

WEEKLY EXPENSE TRACKER

MONTH ______

WEEK OF ______

BUDGET ______

MONDAY DATE ______

DESCRIPTION	AMOUNT
TOTAL	

TUESDAY DATE ______

DESCRIPTION	AMOUNT
TOTAL	

WEDNESDAY DATE ______

DESCRIPTION	AMOUNT
TOTAL	

THURSDAY DATE ______

DESCRIPTION	AMOUNT
TOTAL	

WEEKLY EXPENSE TRACKER

TOTAL EXPENSES

BALANCE

FRIDAY

DATE

DESCRIPTION	AMOUNT
TOTAL	

SATURDAY

DATE

DESCRIPTION	AMOUNT
TOTAL	

SUNDAY

DATE

DESCRIPTION	AMOUNT
TOTAL	

NOTES

www.ingramcontent.com/pod-product-compliance
Lightning Source LLC
Chambersburg PA
CBHW060416220526
45465CB00008B/2908
* 9 7 9 8 6 1 2 8 3 5 9 9 8 *